Classic Chocolate Chip Cookie (page 67)

Mug It!

Easy & Delicious Meals for One

Pam McElroy

Table of

PULP.
AN IMPRINT OF ZEST BOOKS

Connect with Zest!

- zestbooks.net/blog
- zestbooks.net/contests
- twitter.com/zestbooks

- facebook.com/zestbook
- facebook.com/BooksWithATwist
- pinterest.com/zestbooks

35 Stillman Street, Suite 121, San Francisco, CA 94107 / www.zestbooks.net

Contents

Manufactured in China
SCP 10 9 8 7 6 5 4 3 2 1
4500534954

Double Fudge Brownie (page 83)

Introduction

As far as I'm concerned, there are two kinds of meals: meals for one and meals for more than one. Both have their charms, admittedly, but I think it's important to take full advantage of each scenario.

When I'm cooking for others, presentation may not be my main concern, but it's certainly a concern—and that changes things. It means I'm trying to impress (or at least not offend!), and it means I have to account for other people's tastes. When I'm cooking for myself, however, presentation is off the table—often literally—and I want whatever's good, cheap, simple, and easy to clean. There are lots of ways to achieve those goals, but a mug winds up being a pretty handy vehicle overall.

Back when I was a full-time student with a part-time job in central Pennsylvania—and then later as a young professional in Washington, DC—it was usually all I could do to pick up the phone and order delivery. If only I knew then that just because I was cooking for one and didn't have fancy kitchen gadgets (or a stove, I should admit), that didn't mean that I was restricted to an endless parade of greasy noodles and limp cafeteria salads.

With a mug (or a Mason jar), a microwave, and a buck or two, you can make all of the recipes in this book—and most of them go from start to finish in less than five minutes as well. So if you're looking to placate your grease tooth, try making a Gooey Pizza Dip (p. 43). Or if you can't stomach another Taco Tuesday, pack a fresh and healthy salad (Mason Jar Salads, p. 14). And if you need a new dessert idea, well, let's just say I've done the research and come up with a few.

Like a mug, this is a book that I hope you'll be able to take with you, whether you're moving into a dorm, settling into a new apartment, or traveling back home. And like a mug, this book is here when you need it, and adaptable to a wide array of situations and environments. Just be careful not to take this idea too far: If you fill this book with coffee, it will not provide a great start to your day. But otherwise, it should come in pretty handy.

—*Pam McElroy*

Extra Cheesy Scrambled Eggs (page 55)

Banana Nut Bread (page 47)

Ranch-Style Dip (page 39)

Pickled Red Onions (page 35)

Chocolate Nutella Cake (page 76)

Classic Fruit Parfait (page 26)

Mason Jar Salads

Say sayonara to vending machine lunches! Make yourself a few Mason jar salads, and you'll be healthy and happy all week long. You can eat a Mason jar salad just about anywhere, whether you're stuck at your desk, lounging at home, or picnicking in the park. Pressed for time during the week? The ingredients can be layered in Mason jars over the weekend, and the tight seal will keep the salads fresh, if refrigerated, for up to five days.

How to Make the Perfect Mason Jar Salad

Gather your equipment: Wide-mouth Mason jar with a lid, cutting board, knife, and a bowl for serving (optional).

16

QUICK TIP: Use quart-size jars for individual salads and half-gallon jars for salads for 2–3 people.

Prepare your favorite salad ingredients: Chop fruits and veggies, mix salad dressing, shred cheese, wash salad greens, and chop hard-boiled eggs…include whatever you like! And don't turn up your nose at leftovers—sometimes last night's dinner can yield the best salad ingredients, like chicken from your fajita, an unfinished side of quinoa or barley, or those asparagus spears left on your plate.

Assemble your salad in the Mason jar: Layer harder, more sturdy ingredients at the bottom of the jar and more fragile ingredients at the top. Follow the below order for best results.

1. First add 1–2 tablespoons of salad dressing for individual-size salads or 3–4 tablespoons of salad dressing if you plan to use a larger quart-size Mason jar to share your salad with friends.

2. Add any firm, crunchy vegetables such as carrots, peppers, or radishes.

3. Then add any beans, pasta (use small pasta like bow tie rather than long pasta like spaghetti), or grains (think quinoa or barley).

4. Add any *hard* cheese or protein in the fourth layer. Some ingredients that hold well are hard cheeses, like cheddar or Gruyère, or leftover chopped chicken from last night's dinner.

5. Next add more absorbent veggies and fruit, like chopped avocado, cooked asparagus, or berries.

6. Pack in your favorite salad greens. Don't be shy!

7. Add any *soft* cheese or protein, like crumbled feta or chopped tofu.

8. Top with your lightest ingredients, the ones you want to keep crunchy, like seeds and nuts.

Serve and enjoy your salad: Shake the salad ingredients into a serving bowl and toss the ingredients together.

Chopped Mediterranean Salad

Tried-and-True Mason Jar Salad Recipes

Each makes 1 serving for a quart-size Mason jar and should be assembled in the order listed.

Chopped Mediterranean Salad

1–2 tbsp. salad dressing; suggested:
   red wine vinaigrette or Italian dressing
1/2 cup grape tomatoes, whole
1/3 cup cucumbers, chopped
1/4 cup garbanzo beans
1/4 cup black olives, preferably Kalamata olives, chopped
1/4 cup fresh basil, chopped
2 cups romaine lettuce, chopped
1/4 cup crumbled feta cheese

Asian Salad

1–2 tbsp. salad dressing; suggested: miso or sesame dressing
1/3 cup bell peppers, chopped
1/3 cup cucumber, chopped
1/4 cup carrots, peeled and grated
1/3 cup edamame, shelled
1/2 cup cooked extra firm tofu, cubed
1/4 cup green onions, chopped
1/2 cups romaine lettuce, chopped
1/4 cup peanuts

Spinach Chicken Pesto Salad

1–2 tbsp. pesto dressing
1/2 cup grape tomatoes, whole
1/2 cup green peas
1/2 cup cooked pasta, such as farfalle or bow ties
1/2 cup cooked chicken breast, chopped
1/4 cup mozzarella cheese, chopped

Crunchy Farmers' Market Salad

1–2 tbsp. salad dressing; suggested: any vinaigrette or creamy dressing
1/2 cup grape tomatoes, whole
1/3 cup radishes, chopped
1/3 cup carrots, chopped
1/3 cup green beans, chopped
2 cups mixed greens, larger leaves torn
1/4 cup crumbled goat cheese
1/4 cup chopped walnuts or almonds

Crunchy Farmers' Market Salad

Mixed Bean Salad*

1–2 tbsp. salad dressing; suggested: white wine vinaigrette
1/4 cup red onion, chopped
1/3 cup celery, chopped
1/3 cup garbanzo beans
1/3 cup cannellini beans
1/3 cup black beans
1/4 cup cilantro or parsley, chopped
2 cups mixed greens, larger leaves torn

Drain and rinse beans before adding them to your salad.

Get Creative with Salad Dressings!

Don't be afraid to make a homemade vinaigrette. They're simple and tasty, and you can make your dressing as tangy or as sweet as you'd like. Here are a couple of classics:

White Wine Vinaigrette

3–4 tbsp. extra virgin olive oil
1–2 tbsp. white wine vinegar
(add more if you like your dressing extra tangy)
1 tbsp. shallots, diced
1 tbsp. Dijon mustard
Salt and pepper to taste

Balsamic Vinaigrette

3–4 tbsp. extra virgin olive oil
1/2 tbsp. Dijon mustard
1–2 tbsp. balsamic vinegar (add more if you like your dressing extra tangy)
1–2 tbsp. honey (add more if you like your dressing extra sweet)
1/2 tsp. garlic, minced
Salt and pepper to taste

QUICK TIP: Make your salad dressings in smaller batches, because after a few days, the oils will solidify. But if they do solidify, don't worry too much! Use a spoon to remix everything together.

Mason Jar Breakfasts

Mason jar breakfasts are just as easy to make and store as Mason jar salads. Try these healthy, delicious, portable meals when you're on the go or just want something tasty and filling. Dry toast? Never!

How to Make the Perfect Parfait in a Mason Jar

Gather your equipment: Wide-mouth Mason jar and a spoon. Depending on how hungry you are, you could use either pint or half-pint Mason jars.

Prepare your favorite ingredients: Chop fruit, choose a sweetener, and choose a topping.

Assemble your parfait in the Mason jar: Put your yogurt in the Mason jar first, then add your sweetener, next add fruit, and then top with your favorite dry and crunchy topping.

Tried-and-True Mason Jar Parfait Recipes

Each makes 1 serving for a pint-sized canning jar and should be assembled in the order listed.

Classic Fruit Parfait

1 cup Greek-style yogurt
1 tsp. honey
1/2 cup berries, such as blueberries, raspberries, and blackberries
1/2 cup granola

Energy Boost Parfait

1 cup Greek-style yogurt
1 tsp. agave nectar
1/3 cup mixed dried fruit, such as cherries, cranberries, dates, or prunes
1/3 cup walnuts, chopped
1/2 tbsp. ground chia seeds or flax seeds

Get creative with your toppings! Try a variety of ingredients to keep from getting bored, like Cheerios, Grape-Nuts, pistachios, or jam.

QUICK TIP: Want an extra healthy boost? Add a superfood like chia or flax seeds, lingonberries or goji berries, or dark cocoa powder.

Energy Boost Parfait

How to Make the Perfect Overnight Oats in a Mason Jar

These recipes for overnight oatmeal are perfect for people who love oatmeal but don't have the time or equipment for stovetop oatmeal. Follow these recipes and you'll never need to buy those powdery microwave oatmeal packets filled with sugar and preservatives again!

Gather your equipment: Wide-mouth pint-size Mason jar and a spoon.

Prepare your favorite ingredients: Chop fruit and choose a sweetener, spices, and a topping.

Assemble your oats in the Mason jar: Add all of the ingredients to your Mason jar, except for the crunchy topping, which you will add just before eating. Be sure to use rolled oats, not instant or steel-cut.

Serve and enjoy: Either eat cold or heat in the microwave. Both methods are delicious. Be careful: The jar could be hot to the touch after microwaving!

Tried-and-True Mason Jar Oatmeal Recipes

Each makes one serving for a pint-size canning jar and should be assembled in the order listed.

Pumpkin Oats

2/3 cup rolled oats
1/2 cup almond milk (regular milk will work just fine)
1/4 cup pumpkin puree
1 tbsp. brown sugar or maple syrup
Pumpkin pie spices to taste, such as
    nutmeg, cinnamon, or cloves, or a
    mixture of the three
Pinch of salt
1/4 cup pecans

QUICK TIP: If you're short on spices, add a dash of allspice, which combines the flavors of nutmeg, cinnamon, and cloves in one jar.

Combine the first six ingredients in your Mason jar before you go to bed. If the mixture feels on the drier side to you, mix in a bit more milk, 1 tablespoon at a time. Stir well, tightly secure the lid, and put in the fridge. Top with the pecans just before you eat.

QUICK TIP: To increase the serving size and use a larger Mason jar, just remember 1:1. The measurements of rolled oats and milk should always be equal parts.

Banana Walnut Oats

Banana Walnut Oats

2/3 cup rolled oats
2/3 cup low-fat milk (skim or whole are okay, too)
1/2 tbsp. peanut butter (maple syrup also tastes great!)
1/3 cup bananas, sliced
Pinch of salt
1/4 cup walnuts, chopped

Combine the first five ingredients in your Mason jar before you go to bed. Stir well, tightly secure the lid, and put in the fridge. Let the oats sit in the jar for at least 6–8 hours for the creamiest oatmeal… nobody likes a dry oat! Top with the chopped walnuts just before you eat.

QUICK TIP: Not sure what toppings you'll be in the mood for in the morning? You can wait until the last minute to add your toppings. As long as your oats and milk sit overnight, everything will be A-OK.

Combination Overnight Oats and Parfait

When you're facing a busy day with no lunch break in sight, prepare this filling, healthy, and energy-boosting oat parfait the night before.

1/2 cup rolled oats
1/2 cup low-fat milk
1/3 cup plain, low-fat yogurt
1/2 cup apples, chopped
1 tsp. cinnamon
1 tbsp. chia seeds
1/2 tbsp. honey

Combine all of the ingredients in your Mason jar. Stir well, secure tightly, and put in the fridge.

Pumpkin Oats

Mason Jar Pickling

When you're making salads in single portions, you're often stuck with leftover onions (see the Mixed Bean Salad on page 22). Try pickling them, and they'll keep in your fridge for a couple of weeks—plus, they taste great in Mason jar salads. You'll never throw out leftover red onions again.

Pickled Red Onions

1/2 red onion, sliced thinly
1/4 cup sugar
1/4 tsp. salt
1/3 cup white wine vinegar or apple cider vinegar
1 tsp. black peppercorns
1 garlic clove, halved

Place the sugar, salt, and vinegar in the Mason jar and stir to dissolve. You can heat this in the microwave to speed the process up a bit.

Add the onions, garlic, and peppercorns to the jar; stir until evenly combined. Secure the lid tightly and store in the fridge. Your onions will be lightly pickled after a few hours, but they'll taste even better the next day.

Pickled Crunchy Vegetables

1 1/2–2 cups leftover crunchy vegetables
    (carrots, radishes, cucumbers, or green beans, for example)
2 cups water
1/2 cup white vinegar
1/2 cup sugar
1/2 tbsp. salt
2 garlic cloves, halved

Place the sugar, salt, and vinegar in the Mason jar and stir to dissolve. You can heat this in the microwave to speed the process up a bit. Add the veggies and stir to combine. (Add more water if the veggies aren't covered.)

Let the jar sit in the fridge for a couple of days and add to your Mason jar salads or snack on your pickles plain.

QUICK TIP: Spice it up a bit! Try adding a bay leaf, thinly sliced fennel, dill, or oregano for flavor variations.

Pickled Crunchy Vegetables

Dips in a Mug

Whether savory or sweet, there are countless dips to be made with no other equipment besides a mug and a microwave. You'll never have to eat a plain potato chip or strawberry again!

Fail-Proof Savory Mug Dips

These dips are perfect for wowing your date on movie night or hunkering down to get some work done. Use these as templates, and swap in other tasty ingredients that you have on hand.

Ranch-Style Dip

2–3 tbsp. mixed dried herbs: parsley, dill, garlic powder, onion powder, and basil or oregano (feel free to use whatever mixture of dried herbs you prefer here)
Sour cream or cream cheese
1–2 tablespoons milk (optional)
Salt and pepper to taste
Chopped crunchy veggies for dipping

The beauty of this recipe is that you can have your dried herbs mixed and ready to go in your fridge or pantry, and whenever you get a craving for crispy chips and ranch dip, you just mix in your sour cream or cream cheese and serve!

For every 1/2–2/3 cup of sour cream or cream cheese, you'll need about 1/2 tablespoon of the mixed dried herbs, depending on how flavorful or mild you like your dip.

If using cream cheese instead of sour cream, mix in 1–2 tablespoons of milk (1/2–1 tablespoon at a time) until you reach the desired consistency.

5-Layer Bean Dip

2 tbsp. black olives, sliced
2 tbsp. cucumber, diced
2 tbsp. tomatoes, diced
2 tbsp. avocado, diced
1/2 cup refried beans
1/3 cup shredded cheese
   (I like Monterey Jack or cheddar)
1/4 cup sour cream
Tortilla or corn chips for dipping

QUICK TIP: Make this a guilt-free snack by substituting either pinto beans or black beans for the refried beans and Greek-style yogurt for the sour cream.

Mix the black olives and cucumber together and set aside. Mix the tomatoes and avocado together and set aside.
   Start assembling!
   Layer the ingredients as follows:

1. Refried beans
2. Shredded cheese
3. Cucumber and olive mix
4. Sour cream
5. Tomato and avocado mix

QUICK TIP: Having a party? Make these as individual appetizers! The conversation will flow as people will be able to mingle with their in-hand dips, rather than elbow each other around one single bowl.

Spinach Dip

1/4 cup mayonnaise
1/4 cup Parmesan cheese
1/4 can artichoke hearts, chopped
1/4 cup frozen spinach, chopped
2 tbsp. bell pepper, olives, or cucumbers
   (or a mixture of all), chopped
2 tbsp. Jack or cheddar cheese
Hard pretzels, rye bread, or pita chips for serving

Combine all of the ingredients in your mug and mix well. Microwave for about 90 seconds, stirring halfway through.

5-Layer Bean Dip

Spinach Dip

Gooey Pizza Dip

1/4 cup cream cheese
1/2 tsp. dried oregano or dried basil, or both
1/4 cup mixed shredded mozzarella and Parmesan cheeses
1/3 cup marinara sauce or your favorite pizza sauce
  (alfredo or pesto, for example)
3 tbsp. of your favorite toppings (I like pepperoni
  and sliced black olives), plus 1 tbsp. for garnish
Breadsticks or pita chips for dipping

Mix the cream cheese, dried herbs, and shredded cheese in your mug.
Top with the pizza sauce and then your favorite toppings. Microwave for
about 45 seconds, and give everything a stir. If it doesn't combine easily,
microwave for another 30 seconds. Top with your garnish and serve.

S'mores Dip

1/4 can sweetened condensed milk, about 2–3 oz.
1/3 cup semisweet chocolate chips
1/4 cup mini marshmallows
Graham crackers for serving

Mix the condensed milk and chocolate chips in your mug and microwave until melted, about 60–90 seconds, stirring halfway through. Top
with your marshmallows and microwave for another 20–30 seconds,
until softened. Use a knife to stir the melted marshmallows into the
dip, creating impressive swirls. Call your date to come over and pop
in a rom-com.

QUICK TIP: For a richer dip, mix dark chocolate into the semisweet chocolate (still
should be 1/3 cup total). Not only will this change the flavor a bit, but you'll get a
healthy dose of antioxidants!

S'mores Dip

Creamy Vanilla Dip

1/3 cup cream cheese
1/3 cup Greek vanilla yogurt
1/4 cup frozen whipped topping
Fruit for serving and garnish (berries are my favorite here!)

Cream together the first three ingredients in your mug until the dip is creamy and smooth. Top with a dollop of whipped cream and chopped fresh fruit for garnish.

Breads and Muffins in a Mug

Never settle for having to eat the same type of muffin two days in a row. Try these quick and delicious recipes and enjoy your baked goods in individual portions from now on.

Fail-Proof Muffin and Bread Recipes

Banana Nut Bread

1 tbsp. butter, melted
1 egg, beaten
1 tbsp. milk
1 overripe banana, mashed
2 tbsp. walnuts (or pecans), chopped
3 tbsp. all-purpose flour
3 tbsp. brown sugar
1/2 tsp. cinnamon
1/2 tsp. baking powder

Mix the first three ingredients in the mug until well combined. Stir in the mashed banana. Stir in the remaining ingredients until smooth. Microwave on medium-high heat for about 2–3 minutes, checking every 30 seconds after the first minute of cooking. The cake will be done when it has risen and a toothpick comes out clean when inserted into the cake.

QUICK TIP: Enjoy this for dessert by adding 1 tablespoon of chocolate chips when you stir in the walnuts and topping with a dollop of whipped cream or a scoop of vanilla or coffee ice cream.

Blueberry Muffin

3 tbsp. all-purpose flour
1 tbsp. plus 1/2 tsp. brown sugar
1/8 tsp. baking powder
Pinch of salt
1/2 tsp. nutmeg
2 tsp. butter, melted
2 tbsp. milk
2–3 tbsp. blueberries, frozen or fresh

QUICK TIP: Substitute any similarly sized berries in place of the blueberries. And if you don't have nutmeg, give cinnamon or ground ginger a try.

Mix the flour, 1 tablespoon of the brown sugar, baking powder, salt, and nutmeg in your mug. Stir in the butter and milk until well combined. Gently fold in the blueberries. Top with the remaining 1/2 teaspoon of brown sugar. Microwave on high for about 90 seconds, and then in 20-second increments until the desired doneness is reached.

Pumpkin Muffin

3–4 tbsp. all-purpose flour
1/2 tsp. baking powder
1/2 tsp. pumpkin pie spice
Pinch of salt
1/2 cup pumpkin puree or canned pumpkin
1/2 tsp. vanilla extract
1 egg, lightly beaten
2 tbsp. chocolate chips or pumpkin seeds (optional)

Combine the flour, baking powder, pumpkin pie spice, and salt in your mug. Stir in the pumpkin puree, vanilla, and egg. If the batter is too runny, stir in the additional tablespoon of flour. Fold in the chocolate chips or pumpkin seeds, if using. Microwave on high for about 2 1/2 minutes, and then in 30-second increments until the desired doneness is reached.

Blueberry Muffin

Oat 'n' Berries Muffin

Oat 'n' Berries Muffin

1 tbsp. milk
1/2 tsp. vanilla extract
1 egg, lightly beaten
1/4 cup instant oats
1 tbsp. brown sugar
Pinch of salt
3 tbsp. berries of your choice

QUICK TIP: Chop your berries before folding them in. This way their juices will flow throughout the mixture, making an extra berrylicious treat.

Combine the milk, vanilla, and egg in your mug. Stir in the oats, sugar, and salt until everything is well combined. Gently fold in the berries. Microwave on high for 60 seconds, and then in 20-second increments if the muffin isn't firm.

Apple Cinnamon Muffin

3–4 tbsp. all-purpose flour
1/2 tsp. cinnamon
1/8 tsp. baking powder
Pinch of salt
1 tbsp. butter, melted
2 tbsp. applesauce
1 egg
1 tsp. maple syrup
2 tbsp. apples, peeled and chopped

QUICK TIP: Give an extra boost to this muffin to provide you energy that will last: Add 1/2 teaspoon of ground flax or chia seeds in with the flour, and 1 tablespoon chopped walnuts or pecans in with the chopped apples.

Combine the 3 tablespoons of flour, cinnamon, baking powder, and salt in your mug. Mix in the butter, applesauce, egg, and syrup. If the batter is still runny, stir in another tablespoon of flour. Gently fold in the chopped apples. Microwave on high for about 90 seconds, and then in 20-second increments until the desired doneness is reached.

Pumpkin Muffin

Eggs in a Mug

Breakfast is supposed to be the most important meal of the day, but it's easy to forget to eat in the midst of the morning rush. With these heart-healthy, versatile, and tasty eggs-in-a-mug recipes, you'll always have time for breakfast. Start with the necessities—eggs and milk—and the rest is up to you!

Fail-Proof Egg Recipes

Extra Cheesy Scrambled Eggs

2 eggs
2 tbsp. milk
2 tbsp. shredded cheese, such as Monterey Jack or cheddar
Salt and pepper to taste

Mix the ingredients in your mug, Microwave on high for about 45 seconds, stir, and then microwave again until cooked through, about 30 seconds.

Feeling festive? No need to make the same ol' boring eggs every morning. Try mixing in one tablespoon of the following ingredients or finishing off with one tablespoon of the following toppings. You can change it up and have something new every day!

OPTIONAL INGREDIENTS:
- Chopped fresh herbs, such as basil, chives, or cilantro
- Diced ham
- Cooked veggies, such as roasted red peppers or grilled zucchini
- Sun-dried tomatoes
- Diced smoked salmon
- Chopped greens, such as kale, spinach, or chard

OPTIONAL TOPPINGS:
- Chopped avocado
- Sliced green onion
- Salsa
- Crumbled bacon

Sunday Quiche

1 egg
2 tbsp. milk
2 tbsp. croutons, or small sliced French bread torn into smaller pieces
Salt and pepper to taste
1 tbsp. cream cheese
1 tbsp. chopped ham, turkey, smoked salmon, or firm tofu
1 tbsp. chopped fresh herbs, such as parsley, basil, or chives
1/2 tsp. Dijon mustard

Mix the egg, milk, croutons/bread, salt, and pepper together in the mug. Stir in the cream cheese, protein, half of the herbs, and mustard. Microwave on high until cooked through, about 60–75 seconds. Top with the remaining fresh herbs.

Italian Peppers & Eggs

1 egg
1 tbsp. milk
2 tbsp. roasted peppers, chopped
2 tbsp. shredded provolone cheese
1/2 tsp. dried oregano
1-2 tbsp. ground Italian sausage (optional)
Salt and pepper to taste

Mix all the ingredients in your mug. Microwave on high for about 45 seconds, stir, and microwave again until cooked through, about 30 seconds.

QUICK TIP: This recipe is even better served with bread. Make yourself a sandwich using regular sliced bread or, my favorite, a Kaiser roll. Toast or leave as is, it's up to you!

Sunday Quiche

Chilaquiles

Chilaquiles

1 egg
1 tbsp. milk
1 tbsp. cheddar cheese
4–5 tortilla chips, broken into halves and thirds
1 tbsp. salsa
Salt and pepper to taste
1 tbsp. black beans
1/2 tbsp. sour cream
1/2 tbsp. green onion, chopped

Beat the egg and milk in your mug. Stir in the cheddar cheese, tortilla chips, and salsa. Add salt and pepper to taste.

Microwave on high until cooked through, about 60–75 seconds. Top with black beans, sour cream, and green onions.

Hearty Dinner in a Large Mug

Comfort food doesn't have to come in large portions or require hours of cooking on the stove. If you're craving something warm, filling, and savory, then whip up one of these hearty dinner recipes.

Fail-Proof Dinner Recipes

Meatloaf

1/4 lb. lean ground beef
2 tbsp. milk
1 tbsp. ketchup
A dash of Worcestershire sauce
2 tbsp. instant oatmeal or bread crumbs
1/2 tsp. garlic powder
1/2 tsp. onion powder
1 tbsp. frozen peas
Salt and pepper to taste

Mix well all of the ingredients in a large (greased) mug and then pat down. Microwave on high for 2 minutes, drain, and then cook in 30 second increments until the meat is cooked through and no longer pink. Let rest for 2 minutes before eating.

QUICK TIP: Add some crunch to your meatloaf and top with French fried onions (French's brand, for example). And if peas aren't your thing, feel free to leave them out and use your favorite frozen vegetable instead; just make sure they're about the same size as peas, or chopped to that size.

Mac & Cheese

1 cup water
1/2 cup egg noodles or elbow macaroni
1/4 cup shredded cheddar cheese
1/4 cup shredded mozzarella cheese
1 tbsp. grated Parmesan cheese
Pinch of salt

Add the water and noodles to your large mug. Microwave on high for 8–9 minutes until the noodles are almost cooked through, stopping to stir every 2 minutes. Add more water if the noodles start to dry out. Stir the cheese and salt into the slightly wet noodles and microwave for another 30 seconds.

> **QUICK TIP:** Take this dish around the world! Add chopped basil and tomatoes for Italian mac & cheese; add beans and chili powder for Mexican mac & cheese; or add olives and roasted peppers for Mediterranean mac & cheese.

Minestrone

1 tbsp. onion, diced
1 tbsp. tomatoes, diced
2 tbsp. mixed frozen vegetables, such as corn, peas, and carrots
2 tbsp. canned beans, such as cannellini or kidney
1 cup vegetable broth or water (broth is better!)
Pinch of dried oregano
Pinch of dried thyme
Salt and pepper to taste
Serve with crackers (optional)

Add the onions to your large mug and microwave until soft, about 90 seconds. Add the tomatoes, frozen vegetables, beans, broth, and dried herbs. Microwave for two minutes. Add salt and pepper to taste.

Mac & Cheese

Beef Chili

Beef Chili

2 tbsp. bell peppers, diced
2 tbsp. tomatoes, diced
2 tbsp. canned beans, such as kidney or pinto
1/2 lb. lean ground beef
Pinch of chili powder
Pinch of garlic powder
Pinch of ground cumin
Salt and pepper to taste
1 tbsp. sour cream (optional)
1 flour tortilla (optional)

QUICK TIP: Like your chili spicy? Add a couple drops of hot sauce when you're stirring in the spices.

In a large mug, combine the peppers, tomatoes, beans, and beef, and cover with plastic wrap. Use a fork and poke a few holes in the plastic wrap. Microwave on high for 90 seconds. Stir and drain the liquid from the mug. Recover and microwave until cooked through, about one additional minute.

Uncover and stir in the spices, salt, and pepper. Top with sour cream, and eat with the tortilla.

QUICK TIP: For a vegetarian version of this recipe, make a three-bean chili. Omit the meat and add 2–3 tablespoons each of two different kinds of beans, such as black beans and pinto beans.

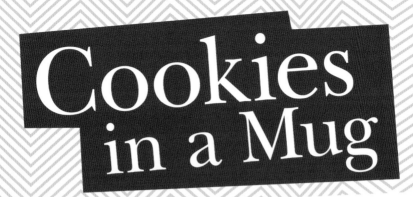

Cookies in a Mug

How often have you wanted something warm and gooey and sweet, like a homemade cookie, only to be deterred by the lack of an oven in your dorm room or office, or simply because you didn't feel like baking an entire batch? These recipes are perfect for the unpredictable sweet tooth: Most of the ingredients for these recipes can be easily stored in dorm rooms, tiny apartments, and cubicles.

Fail-Proof
Cookie Recipes

Classic Chocolate Chip Cookie

1 tbsp. butter, preferably unsalted
2 tbsp. brown sugar
1/2 tsp. vanilla extract
Pinch of salt (if using unsalted butter)
1 egg yolk (add the egg white to one
   of the eggs-in-a-mug recipe!)
2–3 tbsp. flour
2 tbsp. chocolate chips

QUICK TIP: Substitute 1 tablespoon peanut butter chips for 1 tablespoon chocolate chips to make a chocolate peanut butter cookie.

Put the butter in the mug and microwave until just melted, about 20–30 seconds. Stir in the sugar, vanilla, and salt, if using. Mix in the egg yolk. Slowly add the flour as needed and stir to combine, making sure the batter doesn't get too dry; keep in mind, it should be more the consistency of cake batter and not cookie batter. Fold in the chocolate chips. Microwave on high for 40–55 seconds.

Sugar Cookie

1 tbsp. butter, preferably unsalted
2 tbsp. sugar
1/2 tsp. vanilla extract
Pinch of salt (if using unsalted butter)
1 egg yolk (use the egg white to make the oatmeal cookie!)
2–3 tbsp. flour
1 tsp. brown sugar (optional)

Put the butter in the mug and microwave until just melted, about 20–30 seconds. Stir in the sugar, vanilla, and salt, if using. Mix in the egg yolk. Slowly add the flour as needed and stir to combine, making sure it doesn't get too dry. Sprinkle the brown sugar over the top. Microwave on high for 40–50 seconds.

QUICK TIP: To make this cookie more festive, add rainbow or chocolate sprinkles over the top, or use a knife to swirl in food coloring.

Oatmeal Cookie

1/4 cup old-fashioned oats
1 egg white
1 tbsp. brown sugar
1/4 tsp. vanilla extract
1/4 tsp. baking powder
1 tbsp. small dried fruit, such as raisins or cranberries
1 tsp. spice, such as cinnamon or nutmeg
1/2 tbsp. flour

Add all of the ingredients, except for the flour, to a greased mug. Slowly add the flour as needed and stir to combine, making sure the batter doesn't get too dry. Microwave on high for 40–50 seconds.

QUICK TIP: Dress it up! Make some creamy vanilla dip (page 43) to dip your cookie in.

Sugar Cookie

Oatmeal Cookie

Cupcakes in Oversize Mugs

Can't be left alone with an entire cake? Me neither. These single-portion cup-cakes are just the right size to help you satisfy your sweet tooth without over-indulging.

Homemade Frosting

For more traditional cupcakes, try your hand at homemade frosting. It's so easy to make, and always tastier and smoother than prepackaged frosting from the grocery store.

For **basic vanilla frosting**, mix thoroughly 1 cup powdered sugar, 1 tablespoon softened butter (not melted), 1 tablespoon milk or cream, and a couple drops of vanilla extract. Use a mixer or a fork and beat until fluffy. Adjust with more milk or powdered sugar if necessary.

> **QUICK TIP:** Most of these recipes call for vegetable or canola oil. If you don't have either, olive oil will also work in a pinch (not extra virgin, though). The flavor will just be a bit nuttier.

For **basic chocolate frosting**, follow the basic vanilla frosting recipe with a few modifications: Stir in 1/4 cup melted chocolate chips and additional powdered sugar, 1 tablespoon at a time, until the desired consistency is reached.

For **cream cheese frosting**, follow the basic vanilla frosting recipe with a few modifications: Stir in 1/4 cup soft cream cheese and additional powdered sugar, 1 tablespoon at a time, until the desired consistency is reached.

Homemade Whipped Cream

Dress up your cupcakes with some homemade whipped cream! The only equipment you need is a jar with a lid. Pour some heavy whipping cream in a jar and sweeten with powdered sugar (regular sugar will also work, but it will be a bit grainy), flavor with vanilla extract, or use both. Screw on the cap and shake until firm, about 1–2 minutes. Piece of cake!

Fail-Proof Cupcake Recipes

Fill your mug about halfway with cake batter. If you fill it too high, it will overflow down the sides of the mug and make a mess of your microwave!

Carrot Cake

5 tbsp. all-purpose flour
2 tbsp. sugar
1/2 tsp. baking powder
1/4 tsp. salt
Pinch of cinnamon
Pinch of ground nutmeg
2 tbsp. milk (preferably whole milk)
1 tbsp. vegetable or canola oil
1/4 tsp. vanilla extract
3 tbsp. grated carrots
1/2 tbsp. walnuts or pecans (optional)
1/2 tbsp. dried cranberries or raisins (optional)

QUICK TIP: Dress it up with a healthy dollop of Greek yogurt or a savory schmear of cream cheese.

Combine the flour, sugar, baking powder, salt, and spices in your mug. Stir in the milk, oil, and vanilla. Gently fold in the carrots, nuts, and dried fruit, if using. You could also fold in chocolate chips if you'd like.

Microwave on high for 60 seconds, and continue microwaving in 10-second increments until cooked through.

Carrot Cake

Red Velvet Cake

4 tbsp. all-purpose flour
2 tbsp. sugar
1 tsp. unsweetened cocoa powder
1/4 tsp. baking powder
3 tbsp. whole milk
1/4 tsp. white vinegar
1/2 tbsp. vegetable or canola oil
Red food coloring

Combine the flour, sugar, cocoa powder, and baking powder in your mug. Stir in the milk, vinegar, and oil. Slowly stir in the food coloring until you reach the desired color. I recommend 4–5 drops.

Microwave for about 60 seconds, and continue microwaving in 10-second increments until cooked through.

Top with powdered sugar or cream cheese frosting (page 73).

Chocolate Nutella Cake

5 tbsp. all-purpose flour
1 tbsp. unsweetened cocoa powder
2 tbsp. sugar
1/4 tsp. baking powder
Pinch of salt
5 tbsp. whole milk
2 tbsp. vegetable oil or canola oil
2 tbsp. Nutella or other hazelnut spread

Combine the flour, cocoa powder, sugar, baking powder, and salt in your mug. Stir in the milk, oil, and Nutella.

Microwave on high for 60 seconds, and continue microwaving in 10-second increments until cooked through.

Top with homemade whipped cream (page 73).

Red Velvet Cake

Yellow Birthday Cake

Yellow Birthday Cake

2 tbsp. unsalted butter, melted
1 egg
2 tbsp. milk
1 tsp. vanilla extract
3 tbsp. sugar
6 tbsp. all-purpose flour
1/4 tsp. baking powder
Pinch of salt

QUICK TIP: Substitute almond extract for the vanilla extract for an Italian variety.

Whisk in the butter and egg together. Stir in the milk, vanilla, and sugar until combined. Add in the flour, baking powder, and salt. Microwave for about 75 seconds, and continue microwaving in 10-second increments until cooked through.

Top with vanilla or chocolate frosting (page 73) or whipped cream and sprinkles.

Chocolate Mint Cake

3–4 tbsp. semisweet chocolate chips
3 tbsp. milk
4 tbsp. all-purpose flour
1/4 tsp. baking powder
1/2 tbsp. vegetable or canola oil
1/4 tsp. mint extract
2 tbsp. crushed thin mint candies, such as Andes or York patties

Put the chocolate chips and milk in your mug and melt in the microwave, about 30 seconds; stir until incorporated. Stir in the flour, baking powder, oil, and mint extract. Gently fold in the mint candies. Microwave for about 60 seconds, and continue microwaving in 10-second increments until cooked through. Top with powdered sugar or homemade whipped cream (page 73).

Chocolate Mint Cake

Chocolate Peanut Butter Cake

6 tbsp. all-purpose flour
2 tbsp. unsweetened cocoa powder
2 tbsp. sugar
1/4 tsp. baking powder
6 tbsp. milk
2 tbsp. butter, melted
1/4 tsp. vanilla extract
1 tbsp. creamy peanut butter

QUICK TIP: Don't commit to the peanut butter! Feel free to replace it with creamy butterscotch, caramel, or chocolate fudge.

Combine the flour, cocoa powder, sugar, and baking powder in your mug. Stir in the milk, butter, and vanilla. Once they are thoroughly mixed, drop the peanut butter into the center of the mug.

Microwave for about 60 seconds, and continue microwaving in 10-second increments until cooked through.

Serve warm as is.

Decadent
Desserts in a
Mug

*Win over your RA or all
of the inhabitants on your
dorm floor with these
decadent desserts.*

Fail-Proof
Dessert Recipes

Double Fudge Brownie

4 tbsp. all-purpose flour
4 tbsp. sugar
2 tbsp. cocoa powder
1/4 tsp. cinnamon
3 tbsp. water
2 tbsp. vegetable or canola oil
1/4 tsp. vanilla extract
Chocolate frosting (page 73) or Nutella

Combine the flour, sugar, cocoa powder, and cinnamon in your mug.
Stir in the water, oil, and vanilla until batter is smooth.

Microwave on high for 90 seconds, and continue microwaving in
10-second increments until cooked through. Let cool and top with
chocolate frosting or Nutella.

Strawberry Shortcake

5 tbsp. all-purpose flour
2 tbsp. sugar
1/4 tsp. vanilla extract
1 tbsp. vegetable or canola oil
3 tbsp. milk
3 tbsp. chopped strawberries
Whipped cream (see page 73)

Combine the flour, sugar, vanilla, oil, milk, and 1 tablespoon of strawberries in your mug. Microwave on high for 45 seconds, and continue microwaving in 10-second increments until cooked through.

Let the cake cool before enjoying. Top with whipped cream and the remaining strawberries.

Cheesecake

2 tbsp. powdered sugar
2 tbsp. Greek yogurt
3 tbsp. cream cheese
Juice of 1 lemon wedge
1/4 tsp. vanilla extract
1 egg, beaten
Cookie (optional)

Combine well the first six ingredients. Microwave on high for 60 seconds, and continue microwaving in 15-second increments until cooked through. Let cool and top with your favorite cookie, crumbled. Enjoy immediately, or stick in the fridge or freezer and enjoy chilled.

QUICK TIP: Get creative with your cheesecake! After the first six ingredients are combined, gently fold or swirl in your favorite flavor: strawberry jam, Nutella, blueberries, caramel sauce, or chocolate chips, to name a few.

Strawberry Shortcake

Fancy S'mores

Fancy S'mores
(Adapted from How Sweet It Is blog)

3 tbsp. unsalted butter
3 tbsp. graham cracker crumbs
2 tbsp. sugar
1 egg
1/4 tsp. vanilla extract
4 tbsp. flour
Pinch of baking powder
2 tbsp. cocoa powder
3–4 tbsp. chocolate chips
Small handful marshmallows

Combine the graham cracker crumbs and 1 tablespoon butter in your mug, and microwave until the butter melts (15–20 seconds). Press mixture down into the bottom of the mug.

Mix the sugar, egg, and vanilla in a small bowl. Stir in the flour, baking powder, and cocoa powder until a batter is formed.

Combine the chocolate chips and 2 tablespoons of butter in a small bowl and melt them in the microwave, about 30 seconds. Fold the melted chocolate into the batter, and then pour on top of the graham crackers in the mug. Top with the marshmallows.

Microwave on high for 90 seconds, and continue microwaving in 15-second increments until the batter is completely set.

QUICK TIP: Don't overlook fresh fruit! Have an orange, apple, or banana lying around? Chop it up and use as a topping for any of these desserts. You'll be adding not only a bit of freshness, but healthy vitamins and nutrients as well!

Berry Crisp

2 tbsp. instant oats
2 tbsp. sugar
2 tbsp. flour
1/4 tsp. nutmeg or cinnamon
1 tbsp. unsalted butter, melted
1 tbsp. milk
1/2 cup fresh berries
Whipped cream or powdered sugar (optional)

Combine the oats, sugar, flour, and nutmeg or cinnamon in your mug. Stir in the butter and milk until everything is coated. Top with the berries.

Microwave on high for 90 seconds, and continue microwaving in 15-second increments until the berries start to steam. Top with whipped cream or powdered sugar.

Berry Crisp

Index

91

93

Liquid/Dry Measurement Conversion Chart

US	METRIC
1/4 teaspoon	1.25 milliliters
1/2 teaspoon	2.5 milliliters
1 teaspoon	5 milliliters
1 tablespoon (3 teaspoons)	15 milliliters
1 fluid ounce (2 tablespoons)	30 milliliters
1/4 cup	60 milliliters
1/3 cup	80 milliliters
1/2 cup	120 milliliters
1 cup	240 milliliters
1 pint (2 cups)	480 milliliters
1 quart (4 cups/32 ounces)	960 milliliters
1 gallon (4 quarts)	3.84 liters
1 ounce (by weight)	28 grams
1 pound	448 grams
2.2 pounds	1 kilogram